phoenix

rising from the ashes

Lauren Marie Dudley

you changed my world
the least I can do
is devote my heart to you in return

dedicated to you, my love

copyright

ISBN: 979-8-9920665-1-7

table of contents

burn

drenched

the heavens opened upon me today
I stood drenched head to toe
party to loud cracks across the sky
locked out of my apartment
fumbling with a key
just glad someone up there
was mourning the loss of you too.

written in us

can I write us a story? will you give me that
and only that? I'm not foolish. I know it's
fiction. in reality, there's no clear plot
ahead. I think our characters barely even
met. a side angle that should've had more
airtime. the ones you see glimpses of.
wondering if the writers missed a trick. but
I can give us our moment. if you'll lend me
your name. your shirt. your fingertips. if
you'll allow me to run your hands through
my hair. your tongue against my thigh.
your initial traced into my skin. if you'll
permit me to make your corner of the world
collide with mine. intense. eruptive.
explosive. you don't have to read it. I don't
mind. it's fine if you don't want to. but I
think you might like it. devour it. savour it.
relish in it for years to come. can I?

united

I don't know
one
single
woman
who has not had her body touched
without consent.
the conversation rolls over and over
friends
family
work colleagues
strangers with puffy eyes in pub bathrooms
I tell a tale
matched every time
a lover
a partner
a friend
a brother
a boss
a father
a colleague
a stranger
groping on dance floors
hands moving whilst sleeping
grooming younger ears
attacks on street corners

in corners of parties
in beds
in homes
in parks
in swimming pools
in public
in private
in front of averted gazes
the outcome differs
the stories twist and turn from here
strangled pleas
tears streaming
bouncers interfering
bruises
handprints
bite marks
drinks thrown
nonchalance
words unsaid
police interviews
statements repeated
court cases
family disbelief
HR meetings
rape kits
jail time
pain for years and years and years
or not at all

trauma shutting down a body
or a fierce reclamation of sexuality
night terrors
unable to be alone
keys held between fists
alcohol turned friend
insomnia
aversion to touch
pretence of nonchalance
a face
a name
a sound
a feeling
ingrained into a mind
forevermore
these women and I
united in trauma
and strength
I don't know
one
single
woman
who has not had her body touched
without consent.

only friends

affection. tension. wanting. between friends. just friends. almost friends. how many messages do you rewrite. attempting to stay within our lines. what did they say. did you mention that sometimes your skin screams for my touch. even though it's barely familiar to you. how sometimes the days elongate with the vision of my face. my thighs. my lips. do you fantasise about how your name would sound falling from them. more often than you'd like to admit. to me. to yourself. do you imagine me there. desperate. sweaty. needing. do you quietly yearn for another life. wondering how our laughter would echo in the quiet of the night. imagining the way our shadows would dance in the soft glow of the kitchen light. what dreams we'd share if we dared to cross that line. what your initial would look like dangled against my curves. how our names would align together across embossed parchment. what would it be like if we weren't friends. just friends. almost friends.

liar

so pretend
like your hand isn't empty
when mine isn't enclosed
like the world doesn't shift
when your name spills from my lips
like wars wouldn't end
when I wrap my legs around you
like the looks we shared
could be ever shared with another.

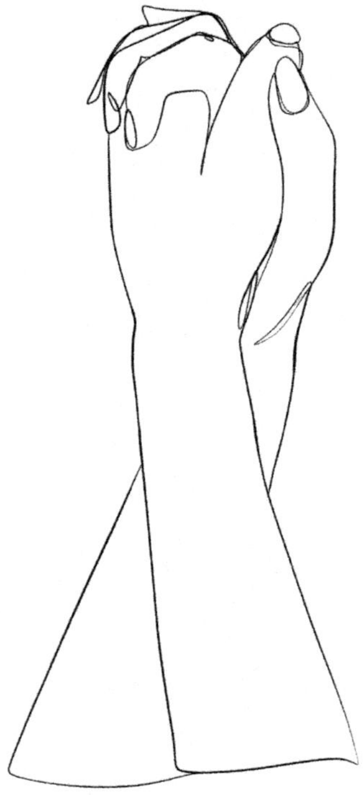

moving on

it doesn't really bother me anymore
it
you
us
and something about that bothers me.

pounce

it sits under my skin
pulsing deep red
clawing into my bones
cracking me open from the inside
it extends along my spine
changing my posture
into a hungry panther
sitting perfectly poised
waiting to bite
through your flesh
and if I can't
if you won't let me
if you send me whimpering away
it seeps to my fingertips
where my quill awaits
dipped into venom
pen to paper
where I rewrite our narrative
casting aside pages of love
penning nightmares
I conjure up obsessively
turning you into
a villain
in your own happy ending.

fog

what the fuck
is my brain doing
and how do
I make it stop.

caveat

'I'm not looking for anything serious', he says.
taking care to place a gentle caveat. an excuse he already knows he's going to need.
you should've taken note, but the glint of promise in his eyes made you tune out. white noise.
a distraction from what you perceived as glowing potential.
he feigns innocence. a comment once voiced is never mentioned again.
and so, it begins.
your name, your identity have slowly been replaced with 'baby' - having the same effect as energy flowing through a lightbulb. you will shine.
you'll watch this glorious man take up residence in your bed, your home, your mind. he'll talk of romance.
he'll trace his name into your skin over and over again.
he'll tell you you're beautiful.
you'll whisper your secrets to him, the ones you never dare say out loud.
he'll dream up trips and travels and talk of journeys yet to come.
his words become beautiful sentiments of a hopeful future.
addictive.
his name on your screen becomes a familiarity.

you share with him the shit days and excitements and
astounding things you learn along the way.
he'll consume space in your calendar in the same way he
does your mind.
you'll drive for miles upon miles, never once lifting your
adoring gaze from his angelic face.
you've found something good here.
you've found magic.
you're hooked. you're reeled in.
you're falling and tripping and ready to leap.
you open your mouth to bravely pour it out.
the longing. the hope. the belief.
but wait, you forgot.
the caveat.
it was there all along.
'didn't you remember?' he'll say.
'I tried to be clear. I didn't want to hurt you'.
you foolish thing.

at the stake

I don't know why I came back
as if the first time I grieved you
didn't burn me enough
incinerating my being
down to the ground
I'm quite sure I won't survive
the second torching.

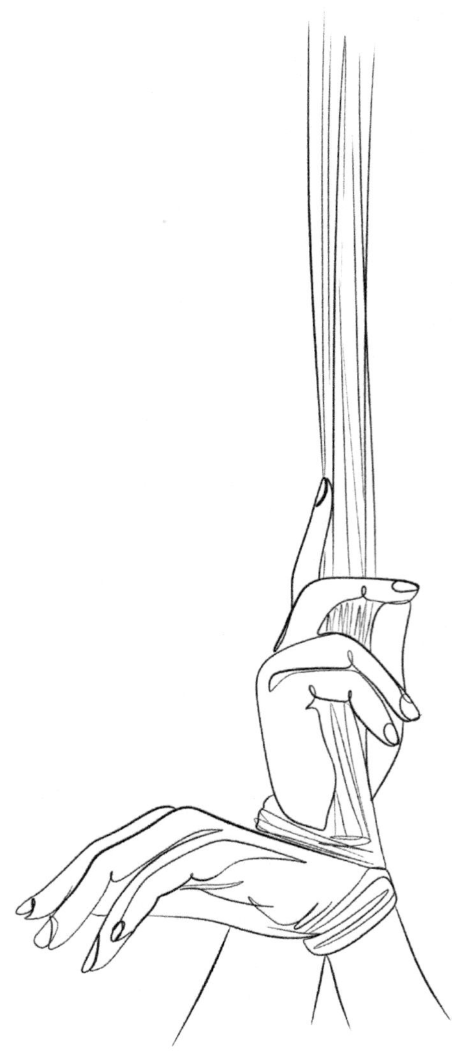

in your presence

I talk fast
to take up less of the space
that was meant
for you.

please let me regulate

the pendulum swings
the middle craving to settle
each end reaching further and further apart
the doubt spiralling in on either side
adding weight to the momentum
smack
smack
smack
fuck
please
I can't see straight
just let me sit still.

departure

7 hours left
6
5 and a half
the panic builds
4 hours
distraction used
lust
so overpowering
there's no room
for grief
just 3 more to go
3 hours and 21 minutes
2
just under 2
time spilling away from us
94 minutes and 51 seconds
how can hands that feel
so naturally intertwined
ever be ripped apart again
71 minutes
under an hour
words planned for days
in the corner of minds
overflow
three words

eight letters
repeated
once more
31 minutes
this is it
all we have left
13
8
5
the final goodbye
lips smashing together
passion
bittersweet trails of fingertips
resisting the urge to cling on
demand you to stay
right here
locked to me
forevermore
82 seconds
fuck
what are we doing
why are we doing this
time's up
that's it
backs turn
the final glance

and you're gone.

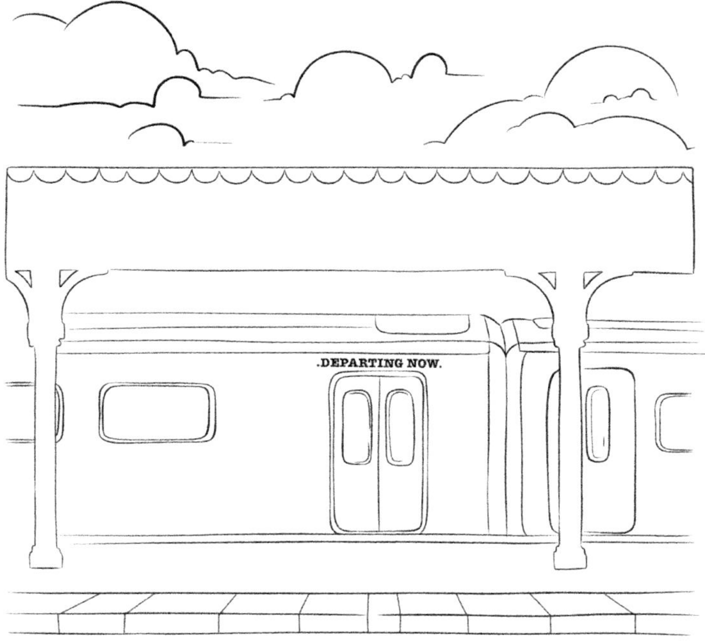
.DEPARTING NOW.

when he calls her

I'm hot
he says
leaving me to "get some air"
whilst I stand
in nothing but a towel
a kiss on the cheek
masking the moment
when he exits
too warm to stay
moving for the door
both pretending not to notice
the coat that he zipped up along the way.

a moment

let us have one moment. just one. I need you to hear the words that sit on the tip of my tongue every time your eyes meet mine. yes. those ones. I know you taste them too. a bittersweet residue at the bottom of every glass. let's design a memory to linger. a full moon. a dark, glimmering sky. let's stand where the waves kiss the shore. somewhere our responsibilities could never find us. watching the light ripple ahead of us. let’s make it warm enough that I can wear that dress you love. but cool enough that you can drape your jacket around my shoulders. someone afar can play an old love song. a guitar. a man’s voice reaching out to us in the breeze. we can sit. I’ll rest my head on your shoulder. you can press your lips to my hair. let’s not rush it. we’ll wait. savouring in it like the first sip of a long-awaited vintage. when the moment comes, we’ll both know. I’ll look up to you. half-smiling. our fingers will interlace. you’ll bring our hands to your lips. pressing gently. when the words step through to reality, let them be quiet enough for only us to hear. but let them be filled with a devotion so magnetic it echoes around the trees. they can weep for us. leaves drifting to the floor around two silhouettes. united in simultaneous love and loss. never to be interlinked again.

yearning

I've spent three years wondering
how it could be possible
that we were on such different pages
how you could just leave
into the arms of another
without turning around
without even so much
as a glance in my direction
it's been three years and still
my mind falters trying to comprehend
how my feelings for you could be
so deep-rooted
so immovable
so fierce
and somehow
it doesn't seem you had any at all.

their rules

you should exercise
you should go for a run
is your bowl too full
you eat so much
if I ate like you I'd be huge
carbs? again?
there's salad you know
you should ride your bike
wine is so fattening
jeans are looking a little tight
have you done any fitness
high-intensity movement
it's good for you you know
bodies are supposed to be *thin*

really?
I've used up all my energy today,
just getting out of bed.

hear me

I visited a temple and silently screamed at the gods. begging. *help me. please help me.* it was so loud I thought the person next to me would catch me, collapsing into their arms. I thought the priests would rush towards me. pull me in. touch my head. nourish my mind. feed me peace. I thought they'd know I needed it. I thought they'd feel it. but I knelt. I bowed. and then I moved along my way. following behind the masses to the exit, wondering if anyone else is screaming too.

disgust

it flashes over my body
as I scan my eyes across the mirror
a swelling hip
thighs that touch
skin seemingly pulling
over my shrinking frame
rolls
rolls
rolls
as I sit consuming nothing but guilt
it imprints on my flesh
disgust.

ruminating

down the rabbit hole I go
another senseless spiral
one thought causing
a violent mood change
gripped
into an alternate reality
a world that doesn't exist
outside of the confines
of my own darkened mind.

wreckage

you walked right into a blistering fire
ignoring alarms screeching for you to halt
pretending not to hear the screams for help
past the brave
heaving others from the wreckage
flames burning the oxygen around you
suffocating you, intoxicating you
knowingly striding in
then daring to wonder
why your whole body
burns.

crimson

you have consumed me once again
recklessly pouring salt into healing wounds
taking a greasy palm to my skin and
forcing
pushing
compressing
those tiny granules
into the slices along my arms
daring to not notice the blood trickling
crimson puddles around us
drowning only me.

blizzard

it keeps snowballing
I can feel it coming
at first, it was a little flurry
an annoyance to a few
nothing major
barely noticeable
but the snow keeps falling
we're letting it drift down
dancing in the beauty
marvelling at it
doing nothing to stop it
they're screaming out warnings
weather reporters panicking
white layers getting thicker
houses snowed in
avalanches preparing to rip
through quiet promises
fates almost sealed
you or I are going to
have to get the sense
to stop
now
before we all suffocate.

certainty

exhausted
our bodies ache from
the interchanging of lovers
a relentless pass the parcel
of the deepest ocean in our hearts
and we pretend not to notice
how each man between our thighs
leaves us feeling less and less fulfilled
uncertain of certainty, once again.

what's the word

I'm waiting for it to settle
the cravings
ripping through my body
several times a day
hell, I think that's an understatement
how do you crave a piece
of your own being
just crave
only crave
it's more than that
surely
"I miss you"
doesn't say enough
how do you miss something
that should
without question
be right next to you
I didn't decide that
it wasn't a choice
I didn't wilfully accept this longing
I'm sure we didn't create this
it's more than that
I don't know if they've created the word yet
I'll search all the languages
until I find one that fits
how much I need you here.

waiting

the power imbalance is represented
in me quietly waiting for you
and you always feeling free
to pick up the phone
and call.

ironically, I was right

I think I'm trying to push you away, you see
telling you tale after tale of unforgivable acts
affairs and broken hearts and forgotten names
laying out so much baggage the weight alone
will surely make you struggle to breathe
taunting you, teasing you, testing you
waiting for you to see the harsh realities I see
a woman unworthy of such devotion
so pure and simple and honest and good
I do not deserve you, that I know to be true.

after-taste

you'll find traces of me on your tongue
for years to come
a bittersweet residue
a taste you'll come to recognise as
your own regret.

tick, tock, tick, tock

I'm scared you'll swallow me whole
if you exist in my world
I'll forget, like many before me,
who I was
before I became yours
I'm trying to picture it
my world with, and without you
without the direction you'd give me
without the love, without the purpose
without the space you take up
the years stretch out ahead
elongated
full
empty
directionless
terrifying
thrilling
open wide with freedom
once I'm yours I can't be certain I'll be mine too
how do you carve that out
that space
that time
that energy
I worked so hard to be who I am today
hours of work and mental effort

hours of therapy
hours of practising priorities
for the first time in my life
I'm happy
comfortable in my skin
in love with myself
aware of what makes me happy and what doesn't
able to prioritise that
how do I give that up without already
knowing who I am with you in my world.

ready, set

I'm sitting at the starting line
waiting for you
and I can't promise myself
I won't stay here
for however long it takes.

when he leaves

forgive me, my love
I forget to write about the happier moments
you might read this whole book
finding only fleeting moments of joy
knowing there are so many more
but please understand
time with you is so rare
I get consumed by us together
I could write a million lines
about the way the world stops
when my legs wrap around you
or the way you repeat words I said back to me
hours later just because
they made you laugh
or how magic seems to follow us around
creating romance we didn't even ask for
I always mean to write it
I try to carve out the time
but then the final grain of sand
smashes to the bottom again
a final second
and then you're gone
and I crave you I grieve you I need you
I balance between fighting the urge
to lock out the pain and

falling into it
begging you to stay
knowing either option isn't healthy
to sink into
using the words here to keep me afloat
I forget to write about the joy
when the grief overtakes my being.

rise

left behind

what happened to you!!! why aren't you
mindlessly following the masses anymore.
aren't you one of us. aren't you riddled with
trauma that clouds your ability to think
straight. did you heal? over ten years of
therapy? that's a shame. we liked you here.
you've certainly changed since a decade ago.
back when we knew you. back when we'd drink
all night until our livers screamed for mercy.
back when every tiny drama was graffitied
across a wall in just 140 tiny little characters.
back when big macs were a viable lunch option
and men were always for breakfast. the group
chat doesn't need a cleaner without your mess
strewn across it. it was so much easier when
you were down here with us. did you really
have to change?

a flow state

I have come to appreciate
heartache and pain and loss
as they flow creativity deep
from the roots of my unwashed hair
trembling down my broken torso
ebbing slowly along my aching limbs
until they reach
my fingertips
and the magic
begins.

conflicted

it's okay to feel both heartbreak and love
simultaneously
you are allowed to despise someone's actions deeply
whilst adoring every inch of their beautiful soul
emotions are not unilateral
you're allowed to be
conflicted.

the art of forgiveness

forgive yourself. for the words you said that scarred the tip of your tongue. for the stuffed animal you once lost. for the time you sneakily ate the final piece of your brother's birthday cake. and sang the wrong note in the school play. forgive yourself for the texts you shouldn't have sent. and the ones you should've. forgive yourself for what you posted when you were hurting. or needing validation. forgive yourself for the time you swore at your mother and scoffed at your dad. for when you didn't know they were just human too. forgive yourself for the rules you broke. for the whining you bestowed upon others. for the privacy you invaded. and trust you shattered. for all the times you sat in a feeling you should've moved on with. forgive yourself for the friendships you lost because you were too stubborn to say sorry. for the boy you loved for far too long. for mistaking longing for love in the first place. for allowing someone to treat you that way. for not knowing how to place boundaries. for the damage you did to your liver. your hormones. your skin. your hair. your mind. forgive yourself because you didn't know better. you made the best choices with the knowledge you had. with the healing you'd done at that point. with the love you believed in. you know better now. forgive yourself.

checkmate

I won't lose this time
I'll move each piece slowly
methodically
a well-thought-out strategy
all countermoves prepared
the price is too high
to make a wrong turn
I know the end goal
checkmate.

the calm before the potential

make me no empty promises
of elongated, joyous years ahead
I didn't learn to seek comfort
in holding another captive
assurances of forevermore
suffocating under shackles
leave me room to wander
and instead, let potential
linger in the air around us
offer me just one singular moment
a warm embrace
a lovers gaze
just for now.

crossroads

in another life
I'd choose you
now
I wouldn't be afraid
I wouldn't hold you at arm's length
I wouldn't wait until I was
"ready"
how can you ever be ready
for something of this magnitude
I'd look you dead in the eye and say

I'm all in

I know you can feel this too
it's here
it's real
I won't ignore it anymore
I want this
I commit to this
and only this

I choose you

that's it
that's the only choice I'd make
in this other life

in a parallel universe
I'd welcome the magic
with open arms
drawing you towards me
without a moment's hesitation
I wouldn't waste another second
sitting on the sidelines
letting potential memories
pass us by
I'd look it square in the face and
hurl my whole being towards it
with as much power as I could manage
finding release in that singular decision
I'd intertwine my legs and life with yours
and there we'd stay
peaceful
satisfied
basking in joy
pure
blissful
joy
acutely aware of how lucky we are
how others dream of finding this
I'd make the world a playground
just for the two of us
spending each Sunday morning
in a different town, city, country
watching how the morning light

dances across your face
and as the months go by we'd
watch my stomach swell
treasuring the journey by
placing a flat hand on me
at every given opportunity
feeling life grow stronger
waiting for our next chapter
patiently
eagerly
with no rush at all
as every moment in between
is just as vibrant
I'd spend evenings in the kitchen
overhearing you share years of our stories
in short bite-size snippets
recalling the beauty whilst
hosting dinner parties for our friends
I'd run out with a hot spoon
quietly asking for approval
eyes wide as you taste, waiting
you'd stroke my cheek and tell me
it's perfect, my love, as always
and the room would quiet
attention drawn to us
as your eyes meet mine
my arms ensnaring your shoulders
and the magic would flow between us

oh, that magic
impossible not to watch
effortless
ever-present
unfaltering
right there
that's when I'd know
in this other life
that diving in head-first
was the best decision I'd ever made.

decompression

feel your lungs contract
as breath exits your body
and with it
we let go
a bad moment
a bad day
a bad week
any and all negative emotion
you can choose to simply
breathe out.

reborn

the pressure rose and rose. the anxiety too high to battle. my mind consumed. head fuzzy. internal fury. my very being felt chaotic. organs flipped upside down. inside out. blood clogged my veins. refusing to flow. refusing to move. refusing to do the only thing I needed it to. stuck. bile sat in my throat. acid burned through my voice. unable to scream discomfort. unable to decipher thoughts. ruminating. suffocating. I threw my own hands around my throat, willing air to gasp through to my lungs. nails scraping the walls surrounding me. pulling flesh from my bones. desperation. building and building and building. I needed release. relief. I pulled myself apart limb from limb. tugging. yanking. wrenching. detaching. I found my tear ducts. I kissed them and comforted them and showed them it was okay to stop overflowing. I turned to my lungs. I propped them back open and whispered encouragement to them until they expanded on their own once again. I untied my tongue. I retaught it the language it had forgotten to speak without malice or fear. I moved to my brain. I carved it back out from all the moss caking it, covering it, intertwined throughout. I spent weeks, months with it, nurturing it back to sanity. I cleaned every inch of myself. I left nothing untouched. I showed myself the love I didn't even know I was capable of finding from within. I learnt to understand I need that. I deserve that. I am worthy of that.

mon amour

maybe it's enough that you're a
great love
maybe you don't have to be
the love
maybe our worlds won't collide
our timelines won't match
everything feels too out of sync
to reel it together
maybe that's enough
maybe that's beautiful in itself
maybe we'll get to spend our lives
wondering what would've been
whilst knowing that this
undoubtedly
is a great love
and always will be

- maybe that's enough.

out of the darkness

they tell us it's okay not to be okay
but what if it's not just alright?
what if that's the moment your mind takes flight
soaring to places you didn't know you could reach
perhaps it's those minutes that finally teach
how strong we are, how capable
how the breath in our lungs is enough
to reach other galaxies.

to the mum who did her best

in the absence of you, I find hope. yes, maybe you should be here. maybe I should've had someone told to hold my hair the first time I had too much wine or wipe away the tears when I sobbed over that god-forsaken fucking boy. maybe I should've had a home to return to whenever it got hard. maybe it's all true. but, if you were, maybe I wouldn't know how strong I am. maybe I wouldn't have found out how to swim whenever I'm sinking fast. maybe I wouldn't have the success I worked so determinedly for. maybe I wouldn't have healed myself so ferociously. maybe it's been the single most-defining thing to ever happen in my life. maybe it's a blessing not many will understand. the absence of you.

your sacrifice

collateral damage
that's the truth
you deserve immeasurably more
than the hand you've been dealt
it's not personal
there's nothing you did
nothing you could've done
you're just caught in an overdue whirlwind
we underestimated the weather warnings for
a force of nature that couldn't be stopped
and I hope it brings you
some solace to know
the decision was not taken lightly
I don't expect you to understand but
as brutal as I know it to be
I believe it's worth it
and I pray to the universe
your sacrifice is noticed
and soon something will intervene
bringing with it the life you utterly deserve
there's so much good coming your way
I just know it.

girl's girls

for a long time, I thought maybe I wasn't a girls girl. I didn't fit the mould. I don't take a woman's side in every fight. I think women are wrong, actually, a lot. I don't really mind if someone dates someone's ex, as long as it's respectfully communicated. I know, I know. don't hate me. it's not that I don't see the pain it could cause. it's more I see the love that could be wasted if we don't allow for it. shouldn't "girl code" be more about taking a bullet for the other, making space for the other to crawl through the trenches, searching for all the love they could ever hope for. I'll back you. I'll turn a blind eye to your fuck ups. I'll wait for you when you drown and resurface from the tidal wave of a new love. isn't that the most powerful thing you've ever known. it's alright. get lost in it. follow what feels good. I want you to. I'll sit on the shore. a guiding light to follow home. and shift shapes along the way too, if you need to. grow. heal. become an entirely different person. move countries. find a chunk of yourself. lose a small part of you I grew up with. I'll help you throw the funeral. we'll dance in black. I don't mind. truly. that's my version. that's being a girl's girl. allowing you to break every rule they've ever screamed at us and backing you all the way.

void

it's empty
weird isn't it?
the space between the fucking that used to be filled with
laughter and stories and love
so much love
endless amounts of love
the kind of love made the hairs on skin stand on end
never unlocking eyes
sitting on the balcony
cigarette after cigarette
learning and asking and needing to understand
every single inch of each other
but last night
between the fucking
the space may have been the same
the cigarettes still smoked on the balcony
but the curiosity wasn't sitting with us anymore
detached
empty
and honestly
I'm okay with that
let it be empty.

the street corner

I'll get the chance to say it twenty years from now. I'll bump into you on a street corner of a city both of us are exploring on foot. other worlds waiting for us back in our hotel rooms. we have just a moment. I think it was supposed to be a hi and bye. maybe a polite ask about your children. but I can't shake it. the words tumble from my lips like a red wine glass balanced on the edge of a sofa. I know it'll stain. I know this moment will cast a mark I can't remove. but I knock my elbow into the rouge anyway just to see what it would feel like. I loved you, back then, I'll say. I wrote the words just to delete them a hundred times. each time more infuriating than the last. I envisioned turning up when they tightened your tie. I pictured their faces. the shock. the awe. I wondered if you'd be furious or relieved. I didn't think you'd want to make a decision so publicly. so I stayed home. I left the door ajar to you in private though. I don't know if you knew. maybe you could feel the draft. I think I forgot to close it if I'm honest. there was always a light on. and your favourite wine in the cupboard. I say I'm saving it for a special occasion but countless birthdays and anniversaries have passed. I never reached for the corkscrew. anyway. it's good to see you. I just thought you should know.

enough now

I find myself yearning for
a singular moment of closure
a definitive ending
spare me, my love
lend me just a few bittersweet hours
lay with me
share with me
a final moment of intimacy
one last time
touch and tease as only you know how
watch me
as my head throws back
as my spine arches
as my body

trembles

I'll mark your skin
one last time
clinging slightly too tight
momentary ecstasy
let us end in pleasure
I swear I'll let you go
then, and not before
you can collect your clothes
hurriedly strewn across another hotel floor

you can pick up your downturned phone from the
bleached-clean table
slide it into your pocket
and turn to leave
I swear you can go
I know I promised
I know I did
but
wait
please
allow me a moment of weakness
let me catch you
before the door swings open
a threshold to our broken reality
not just yet
I'm not ready yet
we're not ready yet
please
I have to catch you first
one last embrace
a taste of a tongue that reminds me of home
tell me you're sorry
you'll always love me
you'll always love
us
tell me you'll watch from afar
remembering how it feels to watch my chest rise and fall
with each sleeping breath

tell me you'll read every word I go on to write
always discovering the raw, beautiful essence of you
of us
just one last time
let me hear those three words spill from your lips
three words that fill me with peace and serenity and
longing and hope and lust and joy and comfort and aching
oh
how it aches
let me hear them
then
gently
softly
perform our well-rehearsed goodbye
the final act in a Shakespearean play
a tale of star-crossed lovers
a tragedy
one last time
kiss each side of my face
east
west
north
south
before the final moment

the last touch

scoop up all the love we've ever felt

in 3am conversations in soft awakenings in harsh realities
in frustrated tones in joyous laughter in panicked apologies
in morning messages in knowing glances in borrowed
clothes in shared secrets in brutal honesty in coffee-stained
kisses
moments of stolen pleasure
gather it all up in heavy arms
overflowing to the ground around us
pour it all into

one

last

kiss

I swear I'll let you go then
I promised I would
you can turn away
go on
please
it has to be now
I won't stop you
I'll keep my eyes on you until the door clicks closed
I won't break apart
tears will not fall
I will not crash to the floor with a loud, aching sob
I will not fling it back open, yanking it from its hinges,

begging you to stay
panicked by mourning still yet to come
pleading mercy
no, I swear I won't
it has to be time now
I know that
I promised, after all
I'll turn to the mirror
and soak
one last time
in a torn expression I've come to recognise
of anguish
of pain and love intertwined with an addictive beauty
I'll open my mouth
and I'll make myself a promise
one I swear to keep

'enough now.'

soon

and still I accept you at your worst
for just a chance that you could once again
appear at your best.

encaptured

digging for fuel upon a fire
that I can't seem make exist
begging for hatred in a second
where all I feel is love
feed me, my love
feed me passion
feed me a burning I've never known before
allow me this small mercy
allow me to feel only betrayal
I know no other way to grieve the end
do not ask for forgiveness
but let me soak in a painful loss
let me be free of
this prison we call love.

volatility

in and out
up and down
round and round
chasing my tail
trying to catch my own breath
suddenly finding myself mid-ocean
directionless and drowning.

drown

it comes crashing over me
the wave I've kept at bay
overpowering
his lips smash against mine once more
a moment of temptation he succumbs to
pleading sobriety
lust and longing and belief
fucking
excruciating
pain
it doesn't feel right
a little too rough
a little too careless
teeth grazing against my skin
marking a territory he's come to know as his own
the answer is no.
asserting the very same boundary I've proudly naively
bravely held on to for all this time
firmly drawing a bold line in the sand
almost daring the ocean to cross it once again
engulf it with pleasure and leave no trace
show me how little I mean to you once more
let me crave you
and that he does
he taunts he teases he grabs
he devotedly apologises for doing so

but don't you know
he's missed me
or so he whispers in my ear
as his fingertips tarnish my skin
a familiar scent falling from him
smothering my hair my flesh my clothes
he's not over me
he's been pretending
thinking of me in his own private moments of lust
imagining my soft young skin being his once again
he just wants to see me
naked
vulnerable
owned
his.
he pleads
swearing to not touch
just to admire
one last time
I'm so beautiful, haven't you heard
so hauntingly goddamn beautiful
I remove his hands from grasping the curves beneath them
only to feel them spring back without a moment's thought
no hesitation to consider the wounds he's tearing open
as he seizes me
his arms ensnaring my waist
daring me to bow to temptation
daring me to undo months and months and months

of healing and grieving and burning just to allow us
this
singular
moment
oh he wants me so
he tells me as he leaves trails of saliva crawling upwards
from the base of my neck
his tongue flicking against my ear like a flame to my skin
burning
agonising
I wait to see the old him
the version I've somehow held onto in spite of it all
but what I seek to find isn't there
in its place, something new
or perhaps something I chose not to notice

desperation.

hearing another lie I've heard so many times before, I
somehow fooled myself into hearing truth
finally
I see it
it hits me
it's been there the whole time
he's looking through me
blinded by his own selfish lust
his sweaty palms grease my skin in reckless abandonment
of any prior notion he had any respect for me

not even an ounce

it's then
finally
in that second
I see him for who he really is.

disentangle

lift my body gently
from its rightful place
on top of yours
sweaty skin sticking
like glue resisting
part our interlocking legs
thighs clinging on
take my hands
in clenched fists
tug them away
from stroking your chin
prize my lips from yours
let me bounce back
just for a instant
for one final kiss
rise from our safe haven
this king sized bed
we made our own
pull the covers over to hide
my naked, broken soul
and I'll watch you
disentangle.

oops

I met you
hoping to get over you
intending to walk away
feeling nothing at all
and instead left
knowing you are
the love of my life.

mutual undying fixation

there are very few things I think I do that are wrong or bad. I make a lot of sensible decisions. I am decidedly dedicated with my time. my touch. my love. but fuck. it's you. daring to sit there in all of your glory. you. the phantom fingertips that glide along my neck. the touch etched into my very being. you. the face before me in the shadows of night. the one that has me gasping for liberation. you. the name suspended in the air around me. longing to be outlined along the contour of your thighs. you. making me question every decision I ever made from eight thousand fucking miles away. yes, *you*. the question mark I accidentally placed amongst even the most sacred of promises. *you*. it's always going to be you. you're one decision I want to make and I simply don't care much about whether it's good, or bad, or right, or fair. I just want you.

essence of you

I read someone else's words tonight. a
poem I almost scrolled past. between
every line, I found the essence of you.
I didn't realise that anyone else had
ever felt a love so pure, so deep-rooted,
so ingrained into their very being.

the road to me

I swore once that if we got lost
I'd use this pen to
write my way back to you
what I didn't realise is that
I'd have to write my way back
to myself.

i'm too happy to raise a pen

I can't write as nothing aches within me
sitting, regurgitating, awaiting
to ruin the most exquisite of days
threatening to rupture my chest
rising like blistering, molten bile
clambering out of my throat
compelling me to scratch at my flesh
whilst begging
pleading
for mercy
I can't write because peace does not
force itself through my fingertips
yearning for the freedom only found
at the very bottom of the ink pot
after howling at the night sky
no, peace just sits atop my palms
tracing teensy circles of pleasure
liberating any residual tension
silently
unflinchingly
dissolving the art form I love most.

immortal

I write about you
because someone like you
deserves to be
immortalised.

seasonal changes

and with the changing of seasons
turns the loyalty within our hearts
once again, the leaves falling brings
fresh hope of autumnal lovers
oranges and reds littered on pavements
the vivid colours of a new love
a warmth of mulled wine brings comfort
and sofas become gentle safe havens
to remain untouched, unbroken
until the frost begins to form
and we hold in the breath that
forms spirals from our open mouths
to see if our lover sticks out the seasons.

it's about time

something just smacked into me
a slap around the face
as I heard
the words leaving your lips
finally.

self-harm or self-healing

I find it easier to write when the world is crashing down around me. when the tidal waves keep smashing over and over me, throwing me off balance and sinking me into numbing midnight blue depths, until I don't know which way is up. when I'm hurling myself from side to side, dodging the ever-coming debris of loss. when I can't catch my breath. when people surrounding me are falling to their knees, sobs so loud they can't take in enough air to scream the frustration out of their lungs. when I see no other way to mourn the end. when I'm desperate for release. when I'm aching to get the feeling out from under my skin. when I can't live another second with it sitting inside me, unformed, unwavering, unrelenting.

soar

I want her to move with me

I'm fearful of moving forward from the younger version of myself. she didn't get treated how she deserved. I didn't cherish her like I should've. her time wasn't peaceful, fruitful, loving enough. and yet here I am. moving through time like it's sand slipping through my fingers. asking for her forgiveness. inviting her to travel with me. I don't want her to get stuck. I want her beside me. in her rightful reality all along. witnessing the way he holds me when I cry. the safe space I know to ask for now. the triggers I'm learning to process. the home we're building. the one she deserved. the devotion I'll show my children. the soft mornings with their head resting against my chest. the patience I'll conjure up when they scream. the ambition and drive motherhood will instil within me. I didn't have enough time with her. so I hold her forehead to my lips. whispering all that is now true. letting her soften. melt. untangle. I want to show her that her sacrifice was worth it. that her tears run along all the nooks and crannies of my home now. that she's found peace, here with me.
she is held. wanted. nourished. honoured.
she is loved.

mid-flight

I always put pen to paper on airplanes
suspended between two realities
one, a home
with all the chaos and peace that could
be housed between four walls
the second, a hope
of laughter
love
freedom
a life with no responsibilities and
wild spirits
where the hangovers hurt a little less
and the sex feels a little deeper
and on the way back
I'll write again
marvelling at who I was
and who I return as now.

sixth love language

there's a sixth love language
one that only you and I know
filled with innuendos, words and moments
that would mean so little to others
swapping lopsided for lobster
dora the explorer or
any cover of that one song
twirls on street corners
red, sweaty, desperate faces
pisco sours and spaghetti bolognaise
fingertips pressing into the sole of a foot
that's the love language I choose
the one that fulfils me
excites me
thrills me
navigates me
steers me home
that's my love language

our language.

welcome exit

let them go if they wish. let them go, with
only grace. hold the door open wide.
a welcome exit. smile with warmth & dignity,
and wish them well - if you can muster the
courage, really mean it. with each step
they take forward, thank them for all
the moments of joy they offered up to you.
feel only gratitude for those tiny pockets
of happiness. feel pride in your ability
to be vulnerable and true and just a little
bit naive. don't be scared to remember all
the beauty you were momentarily surrounded
by, but focus on all that you still are. take
a hit of courage. allow a little corner of
your heart to break off and travel with
them - a token of the time you had
together. it's okay. it'll rebuild. I promise.
we've been here before. we'll be here again.
we'll learn & grow & leave trails of stardust behind us.

living

I spent so much time
retraining my mind
nursing it back to health
willing it not to fall back
into old habits
sourcing stability
quiet happiness
finding my way out
the depths of darkness
and then one day
soaked in rain
in a small town in Italy
I can't quite remember the name of
I arrived at the next chapter
ready to move on
to grow
to takes risks
to trust
to love
to dive in
to remind myself
I'm alive.

if I had more than one life

remember that poem I showed you
the one about "if I had three lives I'd marry you in two,
the other I'd write from a cafe" or something like that.
well, it's beautiful, but it's not true.
if I had three lives I'd be overwhelmed by indecision.
sure, I'd still marry you in one, but the others?
I'd want to spend my time on a ski slope in Austria,
so I can nail German and forget my mother tongue.
I'd want to soak in the hustle of Mumbai,
letting the vibrancy lift the darkness whenever it came.
or maybe I'd study Buddhism and become a monk,
letting my voice box rest for the entirety of my days.
maybe I'd build a comfortable, peaceful life with the
hometown boy I fell in love with at 17,
back before I knew the many worlds
that were a plane ride away.
a few more lives and I'd spend every weekend
at a different festival and forget to wash in between,
I'd open up an orphanage or study to be a healer.
maybe I'd build a business to rival Apple,
or marry into royal court and have fifteen babies.
maybe I'd swear away from technology altogether,
becoming a recluse you can reach only by letter.
or waste one of them throwing myself off the empire state
just to see what it'd feel like to smack into the concrete.
I'd probably want to use two to have babies

in my early 20s and then early 40s to compare.
or maybe I'd have no responsibilities at all,
spending my days slightly drunk
and getting more and more fat.
give me more than one life and I wouldn't know what to do,
but I promise I'd still happily spend the first life with you.

fated

and there
curled next to you
in the open, peaceful air
right above us
the brightest star I'd ever seen
trailed across the African sky
someone overhead
confirming what I'd
already known to be true
underlining our names
inscribed by the universe
I belong
with you.

patience, friend

you'll heal soon. it doesn't feel like it. I know. but one day you'll wake up and your limbs won't be heavy with grief. just like that. overnight. your morning coffee won't be tarnished with longing. you won't need to stand in the shower just a little longer, waiting for the water to run them right off your skin. you'll forget how they liked their eggs, as you crack the shell across the pan. you won't want to scrape and scratch at your flesh, willing their scent to dig itself out from being ingrained in your pores. you won't want to scream and scream and scream, to push the frustration from your lungs. you won't need answers. you won't crave closure. you'll feel whole, someday. you'll enjoy the sunrise. maybe you'll even sleep through it. peaceful. content. joyful. I promise. it's coming. the healing is coming. be patient. you'll get there.

the vow

just like breathing, this feels easy now
the rise and fall of my chest
the dedication to you
the very same effortlessness for both
but much the same as the days
where breath is strenuous to draw
the moments will come where
we're compelled to be intentional
in our devotion to one another
and when that need arises
whenever it's necessary
whenever you need me
I'm ready.

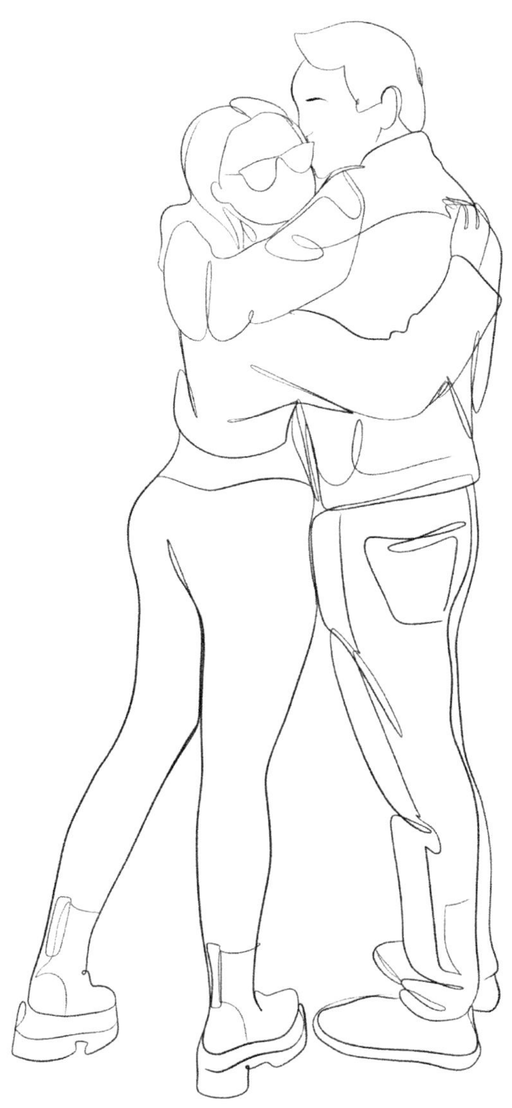

cartwheels

if I knew how to spin cartwheels around you,
how to flip my body over and over
limbs tumbling round and round
squeals and laughter spilling from a goofy smile
I would show you.

instead,
with what I imagine is
the very same giddy joy,
I say
'*I love you*'.

the one

years ago a friend said
when you know you know
and I know everyone says that
but trust me
when you know you know
and I laughed at him
feigning a sweet smile
rolling my eyes back
in disbelief

then I fell in love with *you.*

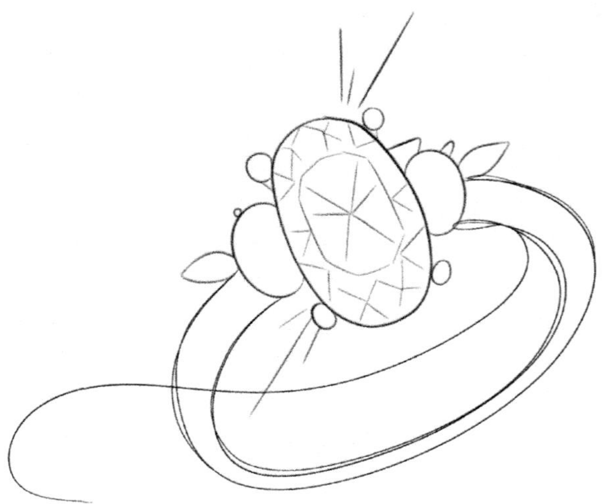

sweetheart

as the sun drifts gently down ahead,
the honeysuckle gold dancing alongside a flaming orange
the idyllic pink intertwining with a dusky blue,
as colours erupt across your world,
know that what you see in front of you,
is the same explosion of sweet, sweet beauty
I see within you.

visualisation

I want it all. impact. messages letting me know my words hit home. black tie events. keynote speeches. inspiring generations. celebrations. best-selling books. live on TV calls. I hope my dog makes an appearance. I want the community. flush bank accounts. a brand with a purpose. deep-rooted beliefs. unwavering faith. emails requesting my advice. an audience that integrates with each other. a force of nature. I want to nip around the world meeting them all. revelling in what we learn from each other. in how we make space for one another. force ourselves to grow. holding each other to account. honesty. transparency. building and rebuilding. breaking and healing. I want to leave a mark. to shine a light so bright after I'm gone. work that will mean something. a life that gives back to this planet. a presence that has a purpose.

morning devotion

there's not much difference between us
they fall to their knees each morning
to express their devotion to a higher power
I fall to my knees each morning
to express my devotion to *you.*

captured, ensnared

I think it had to be a little bit tricky
it had to be worthy of a fight
needed to include a few moments
where I sat there and thought
is this really worth it
am I really prepared to put
this effort in
am I sure
it had to fuck up a few times
needed to burn me
a little
a lot
require deep talking
soul searching
set itself on fire
so we could rise from the ashes again
and be a love worthy of my whole devotion.

arrivals

in an hour
I'm going to fling
my arms around you
in the arrivals area
of my new city
our new home
and in an instant
our life will begin.

choices

I hope you know
you can hit reset
whenever you damn well like
you do not need permission
to change your mood
you don't need a sign or
a problem to be solved
you can choose
right now
to clear your path
and focus on
the bright, glowing energy
surrounding you
you can be happy
not just for now,
but forever.

implications of doubt

if I'm honest
I don't trust you to stay
I think, perhaps, you'll get distracted
become less intentional
lose interest and leave
I give this a few years at best
on one hand, it scares me
more than anything else
on the other, I wonder
if that's not a blessing
that I know this now
so I can make your world
overflow with my love
each and every single day
so much that you might
continue to feel it
glow from within you
years from now
whenever you need it most.
and if I'm wrong
if you stay next to me
curled against my skin
in the early hours
I don't see the harm
with this thought
in the back of my mind

it can only make me
love you
with my whole heart
every moment I have the chance to.

my other love

bring me poetry
feed my obsession
let me pour over
words upon words
of love
of heartache
of pain
of beauty
let me soak in it
I'll read each line
and turn to you
tears building
inviting you in
saying 'read this one'.

happy ending

I'm so used to flying back to reality
feeling your hand slip from mine
watching your back turn
as the clock ticks over
to another goodbye
another almost-missed flight
another call from a half-lived life
I'm not sure it's sunk in
that you're in the seat next to me
another destination
another paradise
another day with you.

freeze

remove the batteries from all clocks
so time never passes and
you and I can have
forever.

night two of lisbon

I dream of recreating that night
rain-soaked kisses
tequila flowing in our veins
as the heavens opened
laughing our way through
tiny cobbled streets
dipping into sheltered doorways
hands never once straying from the others
attempting to stay dry
letting the cold go unnoticed
rushing to this week's home
flinging open the door
thinking we'd scramble to find
passion
weakened knees and
trembling skin
but instead
savouring the magic
placing a dusty armchair
in front of the open doorway
holding space just for us
against the darkened sky
our spot to watch the
locals and tourists alike
run for cover
a safe haven from the storm

letting the downpour
create peace around us
eyes locked as the world slowed
pulling me gently into your lap
tucking my knees into your chest
lips pressed to the nape of your neck
marvelling at the serenity
as the rain cleaned the streets
and we sealed our fate
of two lovers
finally
falling in love.

olivia and fitz

I feel compelled to pen the years of us
every moment, every laugh, every touch
let them to marvel at you, my love
allow succeeding generations to romanticise us
we'll be the love notes of school crushes
passed quietly across the classroom
placed into tightly closed fists
with a shy, optimistic glance
we'll be the inspiration behind an
American political TV love interest
two sweethearts, identically compelling
the infatuation they'll root for throughout
we'll be the names uttered in speeches
gushing thanks yous and calls to remember
as the red velvet curtain draws to a close
a catalyst behind a tale of fated lovers
I'll loan you to them, it would be selfish not to
grant them a peak inside the purest devotion
to ever appear across the constellations
after all, if the universe gave us this
isn't it only fair?

collision

love isn't that bubble rush we all think it is
it isn't the moment two souls meet
colliding
erupting
casting a gentle glow of
pink and orange and red across the sky
it's not loud
it's not visible
it's not that addictive feeling we might recognise it as
it's not only evident in large romantic gestures
it's not the version the movies sell us

love is a choice

a promise

a commitment

love is what's there after that rush
it's the calm on a Sunday morning
making breakfast exactly as the other likes it
it's choosing to stay up to
talk through the fight
getting to the solution
no matter how long it takes
it's a priority

every day
without fail
it's a decision to grow together
and apart
allowing the other to
take up space in their own life
to become a new person
over
and
over again
and promising to evolve
side by side
always
it's valuing the quieter moments
the grocery shopping
the slow dog walks
the traffic jams
the family lunches
the everyday routines you'll build
and change
and build again
it's offering forgiveness
even when it's perhaps
not deserved
it's belief
that the person next to you
is good to their core
even when they're not acting like it

it's knowing the hard moments are coming
acknowledging that as truth
and being ready and open to
healing together
it's a future you're planning
that's going to change paths a million times over
and still, be everything you ever wanted
it's a devotion you make
knowing and trusting
the other is offering you the same
it's beauty in being
your most vulnerable selves
especially in the moments
you're most afraid of

it's a choice

a promise

a commitment

that's love.

life/death/life

after every life, there is death. and after every death, there is life once again. it might be 80 years from now, or it might be in a week. but with every passing of life, out of every grief, comes something reborn. something new. something that wouldn't and couldn't have been there before. a change of routine. of connection. a depth of understanding. of compassion. of love. out of the darkness must come light. it may start pitch black. it may start feeling as though no light will ever resurface again. the longest winter. the darkest night. but by the law of the universe, the sun must rise. one moment soon. very soon. and life after death is never the same. whether it's the loss of an opportunity, a relationship, a job, a phase, a passion, a person or the world as you know it. life renews each and every time. if you hold on to yourself through the changes. if you look through the night. you might find something even more beautiful on the other side. it doesn't change your pain. it doesn't diminish your grief. but maybe you can find some purpose in the darkness. maybe it'll guide you to love. to gratitude, to hope.

tap in

the tide just turned
did you feel it?
it took me a minute
now it's undeniable
yes
I'm interested
yes
I love you
yes
it's real
but
I forgot it wasn't a done deal
just because a gut instinct told me so
I forgot my gut doesn't always
make the strongest impulsive decisions
in truth
I think I forgot myself
and all I've learnt along the way
just for a moment
submerged in lust and love
unexpectedly getting precisely
what I thought I wanted
what I still want
but I remember now
the wave crashed on the shore
and I pulled myself out from it

resurfacing clean
grounded
centred
I forgot I'd already proved myself to you
proved my love was unconditional
I'd already drowned for you
and still swam to meet you again
I planned for this
I created this path for us
I navigated us here
despite being told to u-turn
I've done my part
it's your turn.

pendulum

I keep track
the tone
spilling from my fingertips
I take notes on
which person
situation
moment
friend
lover
is cultivating
which mood
grief-ridden or
bursting with love
it's a pendulum
a natural, easy swing
if it gets stuck
too long on one side
I'll know to walk away.

with you?

I don't want to get married, but I'd marry you. I don't believe one person could fulfil me for the rest of my days, but you satisfy every inch of me. mind, body and soul. I know love is a choice, an alignment of priorities, but loving you was never a choice I had to make - though I would've made it gladly, had I ever been asked. I don't think fate exists, but simply put, how else can you explain this.

you've arrived

sit still. no, really, stop fidgeting. just. sit. still. take a breath. and another one. and again. stay silent. calm your mind. don't look over there. ignore the noise. focus. come on. you can do this. relax. welcome the warmth. let the light beam against your skin. breathe again. don't listen to your mind. don't look for issues. there aren't any. I promise you. no, not even that one. it's in your mind. a learnt behaviour. a survival mode you were taught was normal. but it's not. it doesn't have to be. breathe in and out. trust it. let it rush over you. seep into your veins. stop fighting it. you worked hard for this. you got yourself here. you spent years waiting for it. earning it. creating space for it. carving it out in places you never thought it could exist. don't ruin it now. don't let the doubts win. you've arrived. you deserve this. you really do. here you are. your destination. happiness.

all you have to do now is accept it.

thank you

for you

I had a realisation a year or so ago, amidst a sound bath, that gratitude was the centre of everything good and light in this world. And perhaps more directly, at the centre of that, love. It's something I practise every day, as often as I can, and yet these pages were easily the hardest to pen.

To write a list of thank yous as if that covers all of my bases somehow. A tick list. It feels like an Oscars acceptance speech I'd recite over and over for years to come.

As if there's not names I wouldn't dare admit to myself belong here, in spite of who they were to me. And names for which I'd spend too much time detailing out the many reasons they do, for all they've given me. And names I'd forget, as many years have already flown past, but undoubtedly should take pride of place here too.

People who sent me spiralling through layers and layers of love and loss and heartbreak, and everything in between. People who broke me and are the very reason I built myself back up. And others who devotedly earned their place by supergluing themselves to my side through out it all. People that might no longer sit at the top of my WhatsApp but who's name should be sprawled across this page in capital letters. And those who've been the familiar face on my phone for the past decade and beyond. People who left and came back to reclaim their place. People who lived these pages with me.

My closest friends and family, who have always given me the space, encouragement and lessons to be whoever I want to be. Both the lovers who's names I have screamed from the top of our city's skyline, and lovers I devoted myself to in secret. Clients-turned-confidants and my brilliant team who give me endless support and advice, far beyond the scope of our "professional" relationship.

Lads who I spent my twenties endlessly fighting and making up with. Who showed me how I wanted to be loved, and how I didn't. Women who stopped me sliding down pub bathroom walls and patiently answered the 63035134th WhatsApp about a situation I should've known how to deal with by then. Thank you for everything you've given me.

To Taylor Swift, thank you for every lyric you penned that kept me sane in my most insane moments since I was a teen. You have no idea the solace and inspiration you've brought me.

To my future husband, God only knows who or where I would be if our lives hadn't crossed paths in a house-share in Brixton many moons ago. I don't know how to express my devotion to you in a single sentence, so I hope you found it littered throughout these pages instead. Thank you for creating the most beautifully complex and simultaneously remarkably simple love story with me. Thank you for every single time you celebrated my writing and looked up with literal tears in your eyes after being handed a fresh poem. You are the reason this book finally got published.

For those who found many of our stories written amongst the 144 pages here, no matter what I wrote over the years, for better or worse, thank you for sharing your world with me.

I don't know if I've said it enough, or perhaps I've let it go quietly unsaid for far too long, but let me take this opportunity to say it directly to you and only you. I love you. I feel honoured to know and love you as I do, whatever form that may have taken or take in future. You are loved.

And to those who might need to know this, there's nothing in this book I haven't forgiven, both my own actions and yours, so please know that. Forgive yourself too, if you still need to.

And to you. You, who resonated with my words. You, who read through every page and found tiny strings of your own fabric. You, who just found new words to scribble out in your darkest or most joyous journal entries. Thank you. Thank you for sharing this space with me. Thank you for stepping into my world. Thank you for allowing me to pour myself out to you in the only way I know how.

Finally, thank you to the wonderful Jooneyd, the talented individual who worked closely with me on the layout of every single page on this book, and Abiha Ali, who hand-drew every beautiful drawing enclosed, turning even my most vague ideas into somehow the perfect vision.

If you connected with my life's musings, you can find me on most socials as @lauren9dudley - it would make my day to know that.

And to the poems I didn't dare publish - the letters of love and lust, the journals of countless secrets and mistakes - your time will come.

about the author

Lauren Dudley is a British-born poet and storyteller, raised in London and now based in Cape Town. *Phoenix: Rising From The Ashes* is her debut poetry collection - a raw and confessional body of work drawn entirely from her own life. Each of the 90 stand-alone poems is a moment she's lived through, felt deeply, and shaped into something honest on the page.

Lauren began writing poetry in her early teens, using it as a way to process emotions that felt too overwhelming to carry alone. Her pen became a form of release, of healing - and that same energy pulses through this collection. Now, as she turns 30, with unflinching vulnerability, she explores heartbreak, hope, identity, rebirth, and the quiet strength it takes to begin again.

Outside of writing, Lauren runs a full-service social media agency and mentors stuck content creators and in-house social media managers, helping them find their voice and strategy in the digital world. She lives with her partner, their spirited one-year-old cocker spaniel Sandy, and their two cats, Chuck and Blair.

Lauren believes healing doesn't come from avoiding our pain, but from sitting with it - and her poetry invites readers to do the same. If these pages feel like they understand you, it's because she's been there too.

I finally stopped craving peace
and *created it.*

Printed in Great Britain
by Amazon